COPING WITH Anxiety

ADULT COLORING BOOK

AMELIA SMITH
RENETTA DANIELS

I can conquer anything I set my mind to. I am calm, i am brave, I am undefeated.

Relax and unwind

I am stronger than I think

Take several deep breaths

Anxiety doesn't define me

I can cope with this

I will stay present &
ground myself

Made in the USA
Columbia, SC
22 August 2023

21965095R00015